Arise all you men of faith!
Awaken from your sleep!
All you sons of the Great and Mighty Lord of Host!
You mighty men who once did mighty deeds in His name!

Arise all you women of faith!
Awaken from your slumber!
All you daughters of the King of Kings!
Proclaim again the Good News of the resurrection!

For far too long we have remained silent!
For far too long we have remained in fear!

No longer!

We are called to be not of this world and yet we have allowed
ourselves to be swallowed up by it!

The time has come for us to awaken and proclaim the Word of the
Lord!

For we do not serve a god who is dead or made by man, but rather
we serve the Living God!

Arise all you sons and daughters of the Almighty Creator!
Awaken from your dreams!
It is time to prepare the fields for harvest!
The work is plenty but the laborers are few!

Therefore arise!

Awaken from your dreams and stupor!
Prepare the harvest at hand!

Arise all you sons and daughters of Zion!

Awaken from your rest!
The time of remaining silent in fear is over!
It is time to proclaim and exalt the Name above all Names!

Awaken all you servants!
Arise from your repose!
The Lord of heaven is returning to his creation!
Prepare the way for the Master's return!

Awaken all you children of the Lord!
Arise from your trance!
Praise the Good Shepherd!
Give glory to the Lamb of God!

Holy, holy is the Lord God Almighty!
He is the Alpha and the Omega!
The Beginning and the End!

Arise all of creation!
Awaken from your dormancy!
Magnify the name of your Maker!
Let His praise ring throughout you!

Awaken church!
Arise from your daze!
We are told to be the body of Christ!
Yet we have failed!
We have become too much like the world!
Turn back to your first love with the faith of a child!

Arise all you rulers of the lands!
Awaken from your doze!
Turn from your ways and repent!
For the Rightful Heir is coming back to reclaim His throne!

Woe to all you nations!
Woe to you who have persecuted His servants!
Woe to you nations that have turned your back on Him!
Repent and turn back to the Ruler of Heaven and Earth!

For the wrath of the Lord is terrible and swift!

Praise the LORD all you hosts of heaven!
For He is worthy to be praised!
The Lion of Judah is coming to His people!
Let the whole earth rejoice!

Arise and be strengthened all who are weary!
For the Lord your God will grant you rest!
The journey is a long and treacherous one, but fear not!
For the Lord watches over us!

Arise all you teachers and leaders of the faithful!
Awaken from your stupor!
Your task is to help guide and nurture the flock of Christ!
Do not let the world swallow you with its ways!
Stand firm in the foundation that Christ the Lord has laid for us!

Rejoice in the glory of the Lord!
For He is the Great Conqueror!
He has conquered the grave that we may live!

Rejoice!
Rejoice!

For the LORD is coming!

The Dream Has Ended

Written April 27th 2013

The dream has ended, awaken from your slumber!
Awaken to the nightmare that has become reality!

We have hidden in the shadows and dark corners of the world for far
too long!

Awaken dreamer!
Come see what has happened to this fallen world!
Arise and see what has happened since we have deemed it okay to
try and hide the Light!
Come and see what has become of the once mighty men and women
of faith!

We have allowed ourselves to become weak with hunger and dying
of thirst!
We refuse to go to Him who feeds the hungry, gives water to the
thirsty and rest to the weary!

Why?

Why do we let pride stand between us and our Creator?

We who once proclaimed with all our might and strength about His
majesty and power!
Yet we now lie silent in the midst of a dark and fallen world!

Awaken!

Prepare yourself for his return!
Prepare yourself for the battle at hand!

How can one fight if the tools of his trade have become rusty and
neglected?
We must restore the tools given to us!
For our Lord is coming back as a roaring lion not as a lamb!

We are the servants sent out to prepare the way for His coming and
we have failed so far!
We, who have been called to a higher purpose, have tried to turn
away!

Why do we shrink from these mighty deeds we have been called to
do?

Fear!
We have allowed our fear to overcome us!

Yet we serve the Almighty God!
Therefore why are we allowing our fear to rule us?
Why have we allowed the evil serpent a foothold in our minds?

Arise warriors of Christ!
Take back your minds and hearts from the enemy!
Take courage friends!
We serve the Risen Lord, He who has overcome all!

Banish all doubt from your mind!
Fill your heart and mind with the joy and peace of the Lord!

Who Am I?

I am a sinner who has been redeemed by the grace of God!

Once I lived in darkness but by the mercy of God I have been raised to the light!

Once a captive I have been set free!
I once was powerless over sin, now I am strengthened by Him to defeat it!

I was the wayward child lost and alone in the wilderness.
Then Christ came, found me and brought me home!

I am a believer in Christ and no one can take that from me!

Though I may stumble from time to time, Christ is there by my side!
Through Christ I can perform mighty deeds!

The Battle

We are at war!

The old nature that is the dead sinful self of the past versus the new nature that has been made alive in Christ is fighting for control.

So wake up!

Every moment of every day guard your heart against the foes' attacks! For our foe is a cunning and ruthless one. He has been at this for many, many years. He has no desire to see you walk with the Lord. Instead he wants to take as many as he can with him to Hell.

He uses the wants and desires from your old nature against you. He uses guilt, anger, hatred, greed, lust, envy and many other tools to make you stumble.

Therefore you must be strong and steadfast! Stand firm in the promises of God with the armor of God.

The belt of truth
The breastplate of righteousness
The boots of the gospel of peace
The shield of faith
The sword of the spirit
The helmet of salvation

With these tools we are able to withstand the attacks of our ancient foe!

Be warned though for we must maintain our armor for it to be effective.

What good is a sword if you don't know how to use it? If you do not know the scripture and have not written it on your heart, then your blade has become dull and rusted. Sharpen and clean your blade by studying the word of God and constantly seeking and challenging fellow believers.

What good is a shield if it is broken or bent? You leave yourself exposed! Repair your shield by surrounding yourself with fellow believers and seeking after God!

Stand firm before the enemy and he will flee!
For the battle belongs to the Lord.

Sin

No one is perfect!

All have sinned and fall short of the Glory of God!

We were born into sin and into a fallen world. When in the beginning Adam and Eve were blameless in the eyes of the Lord. However when the great deceiver came into their midst Adam and Eve were tempted into disobedience. When this act of disobedience happened sin entered the world. Upon that day man became separated from God with no hope of bridging the great expanse ourselves.

Sin is direct disobedience to God and his commandments. The punishment for such disobedience is everlasting death.

Light and darkness cannot mix, and we are called to be the people of light!

That means that we cannot truly follow Christ as people of light and still live in sin. No person can serve two masters. If you claim to follow Christ yet live in constant sin then your master is not Christ.

There is right and there is wrong. There is no grey area.

There are no such things as little white lies. There is either the truth or a lie. There is either sin or righteousness, there is no in between.

The problem today is that the lines of what is right and what is wrong have become blurred by the world and by society. Up is down and black is white.

All sin is equal in His eyes.

The good news is that there is one way to bridge the gap between us and God. When Jesus came down to earth he was blameless before the Lord. He faced and was tempted by the great deceiver and He triumphed over Satan.

The people of Israel would atone for their sins by sacrificing a perfect lamb to the Lord to turn away His wrath. Before the sacrifice was burned they placed their hands on it as a symbol of the sin transferring to the sacrifice.

When He was crucified on the cross, Christ took all of the sins of the world upon himself and in turn became sin for our sake. He was the perfect lamb, the last and final sacrifice for us.

He took our place on the cross where He did not belong and took the full force of God's wrath. Christ did this so that we may not experience the wrath of God but rather experience eternity with God.

Repentance

It is more than just saying I am sorry. True repentance is a complete 180* and saying what I have done was wrong and I am not going to do it anymore.

So many times we say I'm sorry but then continue to turn back around and do the same thing. Saying I'm sorry means I got caught and I better try to say something to fix it.
That is not repentance!

When we became a follower of Christ we were to put aside our old nature and become a new creation in Him. That is not to say that we would no longer want to do things from our old nature, but rather it means that we strive to change. To become more like Christ and less like our old selves.

This is no easy task, but rather it is a constant uphill struggle. However, we do not make this daily struggle alone, because God gave us fellow believers to help us along the path.
Not only were we given fellow believers to aid us, but the Lord is with us on the journey.

In Him there is no shadow of turning. When humanity fails He does not.

Where we are weak, He is strong and it is through Him that we are able to conquer our old nature to become more like Him.

How do we do this?

First you place your trust in Him, and then you study His word, pray and surround yourself with fellow believers.

Placing your trust in God, this is not an easy task for us. This requires us to say that we are no longer in control of the situation and it is in His hands.

Learn the scriptures and write them on your heart so when the enemy that is satan comes to attack, you can stand firm in the scriptures and cause him to flee. This is not just being able to quote a verse but an in-depth examination of the scripture. For even the devil knows scripture and can quote it. So this is an ongoing and daily process of seeking to learn more about the scripture and feeding yourself with the word of God.

Then you have the power of prayer. When we gather in His name, He is there with us.

Fellow believers are able to help you through the struggles that you are going through. This happens because one of your fellow believers may have gone through the same struggle before you and therefore can help you overcome.

Forgiveness

This is not as simple as it sounds. Forgiveness is about choosing to look into the future and not the unchangeable past.

When we forgive someone it does not mean that the hurt and pain caused by the action simply vanish. This is unable to happen simply because what has been done cannot be undone. Instead what it means is that we look beyond the pain and hurt and say that I will not dwell in the past.

Dwelling in the past only adds to the hurt and pain and it does not allow for healing to begin. Choosing not to dwell in the past is easier said than done. One of satan's greatest tools is bringing up past events that we have done or others have done to us. He loves to get us worked up so we become so focused on our hurt, pain and self pity that we become blind to everything else.

When this happens we need to stand firm. When you stumble and fall, call upon the Lord! Admit your wrong doing and ask Him for forgiveness.

Christ has said that he casts our sins from us as far as the East is from the West! So then if Christ does that for us and forgives us in such a manner should we not do the same? If we are to be more like Christ then should we not be forgiving others when we are wronged?

Why do we hold on to the past like it is precious to us? Why do we hold on to the pain and the scars?

Let those hurts and pains go! Lay down those burdens and let the scars heal!
If someone asks forgiveness, then forgive them!

Do not dwell in the past!

Fear and Panic

Fear and panic
Anxiety and stress
All emotions we know well as human beings.

Fear not! Says the Lord, for I Am with you always!

Panic, fear and doubt all stem from when we do not trust God to do something and then we try to take control of it.

Do not worry about tomorrow! This is what the Lord said. Anxiety is the fear and dread of a situation that is yet to happen.
Stress is us trying to control the uncontrollable events in our lives.

Come to me all who are weary and burdened and I will give you rest. Cast all your cares upon me!

This is a call to us from God! He is telling us that He is in control and that He will provide for us.

The rest he gives us is not just a spiritual rest but also a physical one as well. When we truly trust in the Lord and let Him guide our path, we become less stressed and less anxious. Instead we let God continue to control what we cannot, and allow him to work through us.

Where Have the Faithful Gone

Where have the faithful gone?
Where are the mighty heroes that once proclaimed the Word of God?

Little by little the truth is being drowned out and suffocated by lies and deceit!

They have been drowned out by false teaching and hypocrisy!
Once we sought solid teaching based on the Words of God given to us so we may grow!

Now we have twisted and perverted those words to try and suit our ideas!
We have used the excuse that it was a different time or that it is not meant like that.

If one part of His word is not true then none of it is true!
He is a holy and righteous God who cannot lie because that is against His very nature!

So it is either you accept the whole Word or none at all! You cannot pick and choose what pleases you and ignore those parts that upset you, those parts of the Word that tell you that you are in wrong are not there to tear you down, but they are there to correct and guide and your footsteps!

If you say well how do I know if the teaching is true? Ask yourself and fellow believers does the teaching line up with scripture? Then dig into the Word to see if what is taught is true! Look at the context of the teaching not just the single verse.

In doing so you will not only be able to discern truth from the lie but also you will grow in faith and understanding.

Anger

Anger, anger, anger
Why do you arise so unbidden?

When you should rise for the purpose of righteousness you remain
silent!
However when you are not welcome you come into my mind and
heart!

We are not to let the sun go down on our anger and yet we continue
to hold it in our hearts!
We have become a people who are quick to anger and slow to
forgive and love!

Why have we become this way?
What caused us to change?

We have forsaken our first love for other things.
We have turned our backs on our Creator!

Why do we hide from the mighty deeds He has planned for us?
Why do we try to go on our path instead of his?

We strive and push to move farther away from Him, and yet we
never leave the palm of his hand!

For the Lord knows the plans that He has set before you!

Stars

He made the stars and knows all of their names, yet He cares enough to know the numbers of hair on your head.

He created the oceans deep and the mountains high, yet He took your spear in his side.

He created you in fine detail, yet you turn on Him and defile!

Instead of uttering thanks and praise you profane His name.

With our mouths that He created we should be saying Holy, Holy, Holy is the LORD God Almighty, but we rather swear and disgrace his name.

We serve a Holy God! Even the demons fear Him and yet we show Him only contempt? Wake up you stiff necked people!

The LORD is in His Temple and seated on the throne. He calls and says who will go for us? What is our response? Do we leap at the chance to truly serve or do we try to hide in the background?

He reaches down to us and offers us a chance for mercy! Do you take His offer and follow Him and die to the world, or do you say not today I'm busy?

<u>Known</u>

You know my heart and my mind; you know what I am going to say before I utter a single word. Yet I have been untrue and unfaithful.

You have shown me mercy and grace, yet I struggle to do the same to others.

You love without end, and I hold on to hate and anger.

LORD make me more like you and less like me.

Transform this broken piece of clay into your masterpiece!

Take me and guide me where you desire me to be!

Turn this heart of stone into one that yearns and burns for You!

Reignite the embers of my heart that have started to fade. Breathe deep into to me that I may burn brightly once again.

Just as the moon reflects the light of the sun, let me reflect your light into this dark world.

Without you I cease to exist and through you I have died to the world that I may live again.

For you are God alone, there is no other. You are the Alpha and Omega, the Beginning and the End of all.

Holy, Holy, Holy is the LORD God almighty! Who was, Who is, and Who is to come.

We are the works of his hand and we are created in the very image of our Maker.

<u>What the World Sees</u>

The world sees a weak and broken person. He sees a mighty warrior ready to shame the strong.

People see a reject while He sees a shepherd.

He has chosen the fool to shame the wise, the weak to shame the strong, and the poor to disgrace the rich.

With Him there is no one who is so far beyond redemption, no one who is so far beyond His grace.

He reaches down and comforts the mourning, tends to the hurting, and shelters the persecuted.

He is glory and justice, mercy and compassion.

He is love and peace, joy and majesty.

His grace and mercy have no limits and He is calling you today.

So how do you answer to your Creator?

We Come

We come to Him in pieces, He creates a masterpiece.

We come to Him broken, hurting He heals and comforts.

We come lost and alone, He guides and never leaves us.

We go to Him in times of grief, He wipes away our tears.

Rarely do we run to Him in times of joy so he can celebrate with us.

He calls us out on to the crashing waves and we tremble with fear.

He asks for a simple step of faith and we are too busy.

He calls us to love our neighbors, and we look away.

He calls us to be the hands and feet, yet we turn and walk away.

We go to Him when we need Him and yet when he asks for us to
live in faith, we say not today.

Hands and Feet

Brothers and sisters are we not supposed to be the hands and feet?

Why then do the feet remain rooted in one spot as if weighed down by chains?

Why then do the hands remain idle and still as though they were cuffed together?

Unbind the chains about the feet and release the cuffs from the hands!

Remember that we are sons and daughters of the King of Kings and Lord of Lords.

No matter how broken and useless we may feel, He sees the greatness and purpose of us.

Look at the front and back of a beautiful tapestry or quilt. The front is beautiful with intricate designs while the back is full of knots and sometimes imperfections.

Our lives are that tapestry and while we are looking at the back, our Heavenly Father looks at the front!

So step away from the doubt and self pity!

For there is much work to be done!

Both the feet and hands must work together to accomplish the task that has been set before us.

The foot cannot take the place of the hand just as the hand cannot take the place of the foot.

Our hands should be reaching not just around the world but here at home as well.

Our feet should not just be traveling the world but also just down the street.

My Heart Is Torn

Help me Lord for I am in agony.
I know that you have a perfect plan for me but right now I just can't see the way.

I try to remain strong for others but on the inside I am crumbling.

Lord my heart is torn in so many places tonight.

Grant me peace Lord, because right now I am afraid and unsure.

Grant me rest Lord because I am weary and this burden is heavy on my mind.

I come now into your presence lord to seek healing and rest, not just for myself but everyone involved right now.

Our hearts and minds are heavy with fear and anxiety. Give us your peace Lord! Grant healing to the family members in need!

We come before your throne and cast these burdens at your feet!

Here I am

Here I am

Here I am Lord!
I am listening.

Tell me what you would have me do Lord and I will obey!

Here I am Lord!

Send me where you want me to be

Here I am Lord!

Guide me with your perfect plan!

Here I am God!

Lead me in your footsteps Lord.
Help me to walk the path that you have set before me!

Mold me Lord!

Shape me into the person you want me to be!

Here I am Lord!
I am listening.

Silence

Take a moment stop everything you are doing and listen.
Listen to the world hustle and bustle around you.

Now try to find a spot with no noise if you can. This is easier said
than done.

We as humans have grown so accustomed to the noise that the
silence makes us uncomfortable.

In fact we tend to go to great lengths to create noise or find noise so
there is no longer silence.

However with all the noise it becomes hard to hear what The Lord is
saying.

When God spoke to Elijah on the mountain it was not with a loud
booming voice but rather a whisper.

When Jesus prayed He often went away from the crowds and away
from his disciples. To a quiet place to pray and talk with God.

So why must we seek the noise?
When our example we are to follow sought the quite areas.

It is when we are in those quiet places with no distractions that we
can focus solely on our Creator and listen to his calling.

Faith

This is more than believing without seeing.

Faith is putting your full trust in to an idea or belief. So if you say you have faith in God that means you are trusting in Him with all of your being.

Faith means that we realize we are not in control but rather the control belongs to The Lord.

Therefore since we have no control, does it not make sense to put our complete trust in the One who does?

That is only part of faith though. The other part of faith comes from your actions and words.

We are called to walk by faith!

Faith is not just partial trust in a belief or idea.
Faith is an absolute either you do or you don't.

This does not mean we say we trust in God and then do nothing!

No it means we are putting our complete trust in God and following His commands on a daily basis.
It means we are going out and doing the deeds that we have been called to do by our Creator.

If you look at a very young child and ask them if Santa Claus is real they will say that he is real beyond a shadow of a doubt.
Without ever seeing him or being to his workshop the child believes with every fiber of their being that Santa is real.

This is how our faith should be when it comes to the Kingdom of God!
It should not stop there either, your faith needs to be nourished so it can grow and thrive.

This is done constantly going in to the Word of God and with the fellowship of fellow believers in church.
As well as constantly seeking after The Lord.

The Lord says seek and you SHALL find.

Lastly through prayer.
Talking to your Heavenly Father daily. Praying without ceasing.

This is how you grow your faith and nourish

Why Do You Run?

Why do you run?
Why do you choose to flee from your mighty calling?

The task was set before you so you could show the world the
greatness of The Lord that you serve!

Why do you try to hide from His plan?
His plans are grand and magnificent and yet you try to hide in the
shadows!

He has called you to boldly proclaim The Word and yet you remain
silent in fear!

Why do you try to ignore His voice?
How can you claim to be a follower and yet not follow?

Why do you tremble in doubt?
If He is for you then who can stand against you?

Allow Him to work through you and allow him to guide you!

Return to Him!
Trust in The Lord and see the wonders he has in store for you!

Heaven Looked On

The host of heaven looked on in silence as the Creator worked in the dirt.

They looked on as he carefully sculpted and formed man in His own image.

Heaven looked on as he breathed into man the breathe of life, watched in wonder as the new creation awoke.

Heaven looked on as man who was made in the image of their Creator fell into sin.

Heaven looked on as the gap between God and Man began.

Heaven looked on as sin destroyed Mankind.

Heaven watched as the Creator cried.

The Creator then left his throne, so that one day mankind may come home.

Heaven looked on as their Creator came into this world and they welcomed his arrival with the loudest praises ever heard.

Heaven looked on as their Creator grew. They watched Him as He dwelled among His own creations.

Heaven looked on in dismay as people turned away. They stood at the ready with both shield and sword to go save their precious Lord. Yet the order never came and so they watched as their Creator hung on Calvary's tree.

Heaven wept as their Creator died, and in doing so He bridged the divide.

The gap between Creator and all of mankind now had a narrow path to the other side.

Heaven cheered when he conquered the tomb.

Now heaven waits for the day when once again the whole world will praise the Creator.

Remember When?

Remember when you first became a Christian? Remember how excited and on fire for God you were? You felt like you were on top of the world!

Then you came back down to the valleys of the world. Soon your fire started to burn lower and lower until it was just a burning ember.

WAKE UP!

We are called to not let our fires burn low. We are called to be on fire for the LORD!

[15] "'I know your works: you are neither cold nor hot. Would that you were either cold or hot! [16] So, because you are lukewarm, and neither hot nor cold, I will spit you out of my mouth. Revelations 3:15-16

God does not command us to be mediocre. He has commanded us to take up our crosses and follow Him!

Therefore be imitators of God, as beloved children. [2] And walk in love, as Christ loved us and gave himself up for us, a fragrant offering and sacrifice to God. Ephesians 5:1-2

A runner prepares for long races by running and training daily. For that runner cannot expect to finish his race if he is untrained and unprepared. A fighter trains by practicing each one of his techniques over and over. He cannot expect to win his match just by sitting on the couch.

Likewise as Christians we must prepare for our daily walk with the LORD. The devil despises this relationship we have with Christ and he will stop at nothing to make you stumble.

Therefore, since we are surrounded by so great a cloud of witnesses, let us also lay aside every weight, and sin which clings so closely, and let us run with endurance the race that is set before us, [2] looking to Jesus, the founder and perfecter of our faith, who for the joy that was set before him endured the cross, despising the shame, and is seated at the right hand of the throne of God. Hebrews 12:1-2

Put aside the cares of the world and rest in your Heavenly Father's arms. Reignite your flame with fellow believers and then bring light into the world, so that we may combat the darkness that dwells with it.

Why Does Christianity Seem Ineffective?

Why is Christianity so ineffective at times? Why do we as Christians fall short of the task set forth by Jesus? Is it fear, or is it doubt that binds us? Is it a lack of faith or a lack of trust the grips us? When did the word of God come to mean so little in our lives and the way of the world become so important?

Why do Christians fear, because if our God is for us then who can stand against us? We serve the living God who is all powerful and yet we tremble in fear. We tremble with fear of rejection and fear of isolation. In place of fear we should be glorifying God and allowing God to use you in furthering the kingdom. If we refuse to let God work in our lives and through us, then how can we expect to grow in faith? For faith without works is dead and pointless. Yet we as Christians are called to have a living faith, one that is actively growing and maturing not one that remains the same. So why then do we refuse to grow? Why have we hardened our hearts against the Lord?

One of the reasons for this is that we are comfortable. When the LORD calls us out in faith we tend to want to stay in the boat rather than face the waves. We fear loss and rejection and we fear the cost. Yet if you look at the example that was given to us by Christ we see that he obeyed even at the cost of His life. In fact He tells us to take up our cross and follow Him. This does not mean that we will all die as martyrs but rather we are to die to the world. We die to the world so that we may know the true freedom that Christ brings.

We are called to have faith like a child, but few know what that is. Faith like a child can best be explained by this. If you ask a young child if Santa exists they will tell you that they know it without a shadow of a doubt. The child does not need to see the workshops, or to travel to the North Pole. The child believes by faith and complete trust that Santa is real. Children view the world in a sense of wonder and joy not with a jaded eye that most adults have learned. They crave and yearn to learn and try to understand all they can about this world. As Christians we should have this same approach. Remember when you first became a Christian? Do you remember all of the joy and excitement you had? That point in time where you could not get enough of God's word. You were constantly digging deeper and asking questions and trying to learn all you possibly could.

Today that is sadly not the case. As Christians we are called to be constantly in the word of God digging deeper and studying it. However so many Christians now rely solely on the church to provide all of their spiritual feedings for the week. If you were to only eat once or twice a week, you would starve and never grow. In this same way if you only receive your fill of the Word twice a week then how do you expect to grow spiritually? The answer is you can't. you will then be spiritually starving yourself and that leaves you vulnerable.

Called

Alone in darkness there I stood

Blind to all around me

Deaf to all that surrounded me

Alone in the depths of sin

Not knowing the state of depravity I was in

At first a whisper reached my ear

A kind and gentle voice I began to hear

Then a little light began to appear

Growing brighter as it drew near

In this light was a man

He walked closer and held out his hand

All the while calling my name

Whispering you're the reason I came

As we stood face to face

He told me of unending grace

He spoke of a peace that I had never known

He showed me my eternal home

He talked of joy and he talked of strife

He mentioned more than once eternal life

He showed me the spots where they placed the nails

There He demonstrated a love that never fails

High on a tree made of two beams of wood

He said it is finished

Then he made his promise good

Faith and the Cave

Imagine a cave that is long and deep enough that light from outside cannot reach the wall.

In this cave are men who are chained in a way where they can neither look left or right and must remain seated.

These men have been chained here since birth and have never left the cave.

Behind and high above the men is a fire with a walk way in front of it.

On the walkway various people and animals go by and in doing so they cast a shadow on to the wall that the chained men are forced to stare at.

The noise from these travelers and animals bounce off the wall in an echo.

The men invent a game of who can name the thing the quickest.

Among them one is considered the wisest because he is almost always the first to guess the sound or the object.

Suddenly one day a stranger comes down and removes the chains from one of the men and takes him out of the cave. The man who has known nothing but the dim light of the cave screams at the brightness of the sun.

He longs to return to the cave because of this pain. However he is forced to remain outside of the cave.

As time goes by his eyes adjust and he starts to look around him.

He sees the shadow of a horse and calls it a horse.

He is told that it is the horse's shadow and not a horse.

He then hears an echo and is told the truth of what it is.

The man begins to realize what he thought was true is not the truth.

Then after sometime that same man is dragged back into the cave and chained back up.

This time he is considered a fool because the others do not believe that the shadows are only shadows and the echoes are only echoes.

The allegory of the cave has some very interesting parallels to Christianity.

First you have the men who dwell in darkness not by their own choice but rather they are prisoners. The shadows and echoes are the things that the devil used to deceive and hinder us. While in sin they do not know the truth so to them it is truth.

Then Christ comes and brings you to the light, he brings you up out of the cave

The pain and sorrow we feel when we realize our sins and the holiness of God.

He then reveals the truth of His word and shows you the schemes of the devil for what they really are.

Here is where the ending differs slightly. Instead of being forced back into the cave and chained up again. The person goes willingly. Down he goes and he begins to spread the word of Jesus and tells the others that those shadows are not the truth. The man offers to unchain the men and take them to the truth.

The others then make the decision to stay or go.

We are called to be in the world yet not of the world. We are called to bring the light of Christ into the dark cave that is the world. It is not up to us to drag people out kicking and screaming. We share the truth and it is then up to the person whether or not to receive it.

Behold!

The night has ended and the dawn has come!

Look now at what man has become!

A prideful and sinful being, one who is not content with owning everything he is seeing.

He can't satisfy the void in his soul. It remains inside him like a never ending hole.

This bottomless pit devours all things that are put in.

It's burning depths destroy everything within.

This hole cannot be filled by unending wealth. It cannot be filled with things found on the shelf.

It cannot be filled by the ones we love. It can only be filled by Him who rules in love.

This hole that sits in every heart was not intended to be there at the start.

In the beginning we walked hand in hand, with Him who made every piece of land.

Then one day a serpent came along. He tricked us into doing the first wrong.

Now we have the hole in us. This pit so wide it divides us.

It separates us From Him.

The One who can't bear sin.

He wept and cried as He looked across the great divide.

He planned to bring us back once again to His side.

He sent to us His only son.

The one who was with Him since time had begun.

This perfect and spotless lamb came as a gift from the great I Am.

He took our place up on a cross, to bring home the lost.

To help bring us back to the Father's side. Once and for all He bridged the great divide.

Precious child

Precious child why do you cry?

Why do you strive to carry the world on your shoulders?

I am here, beside you ask and I will lift this weight from you!

Come to me and I shall wipe away your tears.

I will hold you in my arms to calm your fears.

In my arms no one can harm you.

Draw near to me and I will draw near to you.

Call out to me and I will answer you.

Though storms may rage and thunder roll, you will never be alone.

My love for you knows no end.

I gave up my life so you could live.

A life with freedom from sin.

I Told You

I told you to love your neighbor

Yet you have hardened your hearts

I asked you to follow

Yet you remain in fear

I sent you to share the gospel

yet you cower in the dark

I asked you to feed my sheep

You give the rocks instead

I told you tend my flock

Yet they wander alone in the dark

I told to love me with all your heart body and soul

Instead you worship things made of plastic metal and gold

I called you to take care of the widows and orphans

Yet you have left them all alone

I call you to draw closer to me and walk with me along this narrow
road

You have decided the path is easier with the crowds

I whisper to you and call your name

You ignore me and profane my name

Oh child if only you would walk this path I want for you.

A path that helps you become who you were meant to be

Instead of the one the world wants you to see

Come home child return to me

I your father am waiting

Right here where I have always been

Who Are You?

Who are you, oh man?

Did you create the world with your own hands?

Did you calm the raging seas?

Do you hold the heavens in your hands?

Do you know the number of all the grains of sand?

Can you give life to a piece of clay?

Do you hold the power to give one more day?

Do you know every star and galaxy by their names?

Can you number the hairs on your head?

Can you give life back to the dead?

You oh man can not do these things.

So why do you think you can save yourself from hell's fiery rings?

No amount of work or good deeds can outweigh the sin to which you
so desperately cling.

No amount of money or power can pave the way.

No achievement or awards earns you everlasting life.

The sin drags down into those dark depths.

It takes all you have until there is nothing left.

I am the one who can save you!

I am the way to everlasting life.

I am the one who is calling you.

I am the one who gives you life.

I call your name and offer you salvation.

I call your name and offer you grace.

I call your name and offer peace and forgiveness.

Will you call my name and be called mine?

Will you leave your past life for the one I have in mind?

Will you repent from the old and be born in the new.

Will you let me in or will you just walk away?

Oh Death

O death where is your sting?

O grave where is your victory?

Your kingdom is overthrown.

The veil has been torn.

Your prisoners have been ransomed.

Your captives have all been set free.

The chains that bound man are broken.

Sin's power no longer holds sway.

Holy blood shed for all.

Holiness took on the guilt and shame.

Love took the whip and bore the thorns.

Grace said forgive them when He was mocked and scorned

The creator saved His creations

The shepherd gave all for His flock

Leap for joy oh feet for he has removed the chains!

Sing praise oh tongue and lips for His name alone is worthy of your praise

Therefore clap loudly with crashing cymbal and banging drum oh hands for the King is coming back to claim His throne.

Worship the creator oh Heavens.

Praise the King all you sons and daughters

Magnify His name all you fathers and mothers

Storms

I have called you on to the water, to walk in faith with me.

You look in fear, remaining in the boat frightened by the waves and the perceived unknown.

Why do you fear these?

Didn't I, your Heavenly Father, create the waves and skies?

Do they not obey my every command?

The storms and trials of this life try to drown out my voice which is gently calling for you.

Have faith child of mine.

The storms cannot tear you from my arms and the trials can never make me stop loving you.

The very air you breathe is the breath I breathed into you while you were still in the womb.

My love for you is farther than the east is from the west.

Hear Me

Children hear my voice and head my commands!

I commanded you to love your neighbor!

I commanded that you take care of the widow and the orphans.

I asked you to lift up the down trodden

I told you to turn the other cheek.

I told you that you would be hated by the world because you are a part of me.

I left you on this earth to be witnesses and show the love that I have for you!

I gave you the hands to help and the feet to go.

I gave you the spirit to help you and strengthen you.

I fill you with love so that you may love.

I gave you my heart so you would show compassion!

Why then do you not do these things?

Why then do your neighbors go hungry and cold?

Why do your feet remain rooted?

Why then do your hands remain idle?

The Man and the Moon

A man decided to talk with the moon one night as it slowly sailed across the evening sky.

"Moon," he said. "Are you lonely up there in the empty vastness of space?"

The moon replied with a small chuckle, "space is not empty at all though it is vast"

"Out here there are more stars and planets than anyone can count, more galaxies and universes than anyone could dream!"

The man replied "what about love?"

The moon sat there pondering the question and then replied "how many people are there on earth?"

To which the man replied "billions"

The moon then said "Could you recall all of their names? Could you know all of their hurts and pains? Could you breathe life into a lump of clay? Would you give yourself up so all could be saved?"

The man answered with a shake of his head, "all of these things I could not do".

The moon replied "Then let me tell you about love. Love knows everyone's name not just on earth but all the stars and planets as well! Every galaxy and universe to every little microscopic cell, Love knows every name. Love listens to every hurt and pain, love comforts those who have lost and celebrates with those who have gained. Love went to a cross so all may be saved."

The man was amazed with the answer and said "How do you know this, where is your proof?"

The moon smiled and whispered "All of Love's creation sings out His name, we all speak and glorify his name. Even you oh man bear Love's mark. The breath you breathe came first from His lungs! Just like I reflect the sun, so can you reflect His love."

The man replied "Who is Love, and what do you mean by all these things?"

The moon softly said with a reverence in its voice "He is the Creator of all, the bread of life, the conqueror of death, He is the groom who is awaiting his bride, and He is the one who will never leave your side. His name is Emanuel, I am, king of kings, lord of lords, Father, Jesus Christ."

With that last statement the moon had set, leaving the man to sit and ponder all that he had heard.

For the rest his life the man thought about what was said and finally he began to understand. The day he died he met Love, who, then greeted him with open arms.

Why Do You Tremble?

Why do you stand still and tremble

I have called you to be my hands and feet.

You have remained rooted in fear

I call you on to the waves and you remain in the boat.

The waves obey my command so there is no need to fear them

I have called you to the ends of the earth yet you try to flee

You cannot run from me

You have asked for my guidance and then turn a deaf ear to the answer.

The plans I have for you are better

I have called you to love your neighbor yet you leave them cold in the street.

I call you to be the light yet you try to hide

Why hide what I gave you to share

I call you to surrender and you resist with all your might.

With your surrender I complete my work in you

With my death I broke the chains that bound you in fear and death.

I took your place so you could live with me.

Therefore Arise!

Fear not for I am with you

Set your feet upon the path and follow my voice "And your ears shall hear a word behind you, saying, "This is the way, walk in it," when you turn to the right or when you turn to the left. (Isaiah 30:21 ESV)"

Heed my words and instructions

Be my hands and feet in this world

Be the light that you were made to be

The Tree

On a hill where three trees stood

Sin was defeated by good

Grace so amazing

It counted no cost

The final payment was the cross

The slave was redeemed

And the captive was freed

Ransomed by Him, both you and me

He came to earth as the final lamb

So we could join the great I Am.

The price for sin was so steep

Yet His love and grace ran deep

Deeper than the cost of sin

He died on earth to welcome us in.

To greet us as we come home

To stand and worship at His throne.

The King who came to save

Even the lowest of slaves

He gave up all he knew

So that we all could be made new

Three trees stood on that hill

A king hung in the middle

With sin on either side

One repented while the other mocked and died.

On this tree made of two pieces of wood.

The Creator defeated death for good.

The final lamb has freed us all

Now we must answer His call.

Do we repent and say I am wrong

Or do we join in with the mocking throng?

Hear My Cries

Hear me oh God I pray!

Please hear my cries.

I'm in anguish oh Lord

And I need your help.

What was once may be no more, but it has become more than just two lives but many.

Protect them God for they are innocent in this battle. Surround them Lord with your angels and protect them from all harm.

Soften the hearts of those involved oh Lord. Bring them back to you in a mighty way. Save them Lord from what has happened and what can happen.

Strengthen me oh Lord so I may do your will. Comfort me God so I may comfort others.

I lay my burdens at the foot of your throne God. I put my faith in your perfect plan.

Allow us to rest in your presence Lord in the peace and comfort of You.

Lord we call upon your name and you hear the cries of your people. Grant us wisdom for what lies ahead. Allow us to see your hand as we walk through this dark valley.

We cast our cares our worries and our doubts at your feet, God. Remain steadfast in your love as we cling to you.

Falling Apart

It's all falling apart; my world is crashing in around me.

I try to do the right thing and it turns around and bites me.

I think I am doing well but it just all goes to hell.

I feel for every step forward I take, I am taking two steps back.

I have only wandered farther off track.

Help me God for I am lost.

Guide me Lord to where I belong

Heal me Savior; restore me to your side.

Take away my pride, my hate, my fear and replace it with Your humility, Your love and Your peace.

Take this heart that is hard, broken and stubborn. Transform it into a heart that is one that burns and yearns for you.

I praise Your name in the midst of this storm. May I never cease to praise you for all that you have done.

Prepare

Prepare all you cities of the earth!

Prepare for the rightful King's return!

The blood of the innocent and the saints are on your hands!

You proud cities who have condemned His children to death!

These very children who were persecuted and killed, now cry for vengeance and The Lord has heard their pleas!

You proud cities who slander and curse His holy name!

Turn away from your pride!

Turn back to Him!

The rightful Ruler is coming!

Be warned all you proud people!

Judgement is not reserved for few but for all of mankind!

All of your deeds great and terrible will be brought to the light!

Beware rulers of the earth!

You have set laws in place to try and remove Him from His inheritance!

You leaders who sentenced His people to death!

He is coming back to His people!

Be warned for there is stored a fearful and vengeful wrath that is waiting to be released upon the world!

The Lords righteous and holy anger will be brought forth!

Hold fast all you sons and daughters of Zion!

Stand fast in the coming storm!

All you men and women of faith prepare for the return of The Lord!

Made in the USA
San Bernardino, CA
09 May 2016